BUTTER

LIFE CYCLES

Words in **bold** can be found in the glossary on page 24.

©2018

Written by:
Grace Jones

Edited by:
Gemma McMullen

Designed by:
Matt Rumbelow

BUTTERFLY

Page 4	What is a Life Cycle?
Page 5	What is a Butterfly?
Page 6	Eggs
Page 8	Caterpillars
Page 10	Growing Caterpillars
Page 12	Changing Caterpillars
Page 14	Butterflies
Page 16	Brilliant Butterflies
Page 18	Looking for Food
Page 20	World Record Breakers
Page 22	Life Cycle of a Butterfly
Page 23	Get Exploring!
Page 24	Glossary and Index

WHAT IS A LIFE CYCLE?

All animals and humans go through different stages of their life as they grow and change. This is called a life cycle.

WHAT IS A BUTTERFLY?

A butterfly is an **insect**. It has four wings, which it uses to fly, two eyes and six legs.

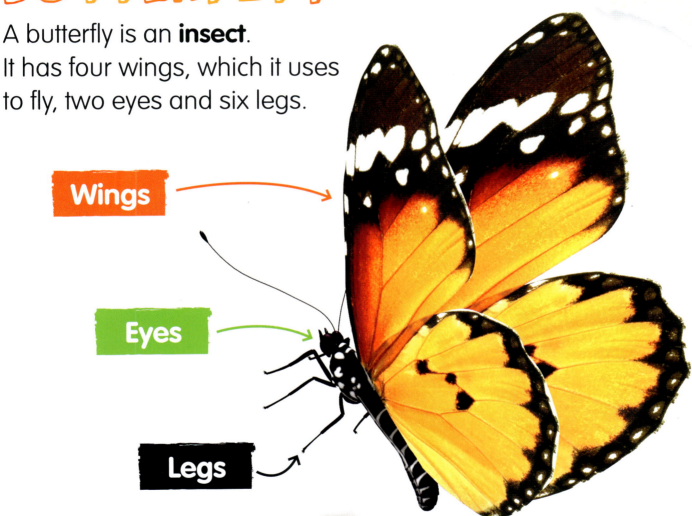

Wings

Eyes

Legs

EGGS

A butterfly finds a plant to lay her eggs on. She sticks her eggs to the plant's leaves with a special sort of glue that she makes.

Butterfly Eggs

Some butterflies lay over one hundred eggs at a time. Their eggs can be many different colours, shapes and sizes.

CATERPILLARS

Caterpillar

Egg Shell

A butterfly's eggs usually **hatch** after around one week. The hungry caterpillars chew holes in their eggshells to wriggle out of.

Caterpillars have twelve eyes and six legs. Some caterpillars are brightly coloured, some have stripes and some are hairy!

GROWING CATERPILLARS

The caterpillar is very hungry and eats the leaves around it for food. It needs a lot of food to grow big and strong.

A caterpillar will shed its skin around five times when it is growing.

A caterpillar's old skin.

The caterpillar grows so quickly that its skin gets too tight for its body. It **sheds** its old skin and grows a new, bigger skin underneath.

CHANGING CATERPILLARS

Once the caterpillar has grown enough, it makes a hard shell around its soft body. This is called a **chrysalis**.

Inside the chrysalis, the caterpillar changes into a butterfly. The chrysalis often changes colour as the caterpillar turns into a butterfly.

BUTTERFLIES

When the caterpillar is ready, the chrysalis breaks open and a butterfly comes out.

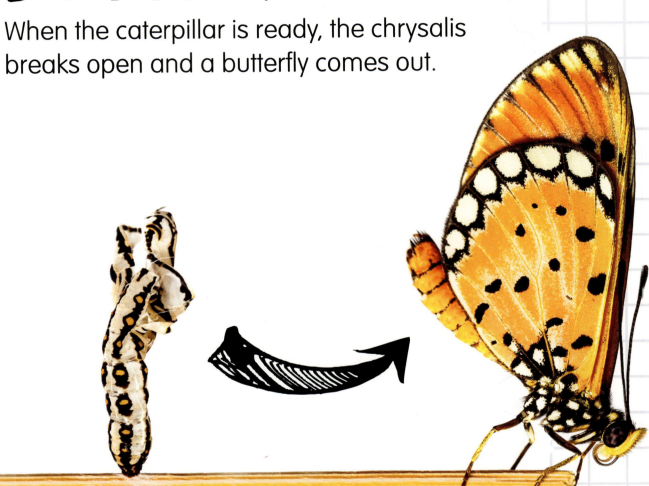

Chrysalis

Butterfly

The butterfly rests its body and waits for its wings to dry. Once it has rested, it flies away to look for food.

BRILLIANT BUTTERFLIES

Butterflies' wings can be colourful and can have lots of different patterns on them.

Ulysses Butterfly

The Leaf butterfly looks like a dead leaf when its wings are together. This helps it to hide from other animals who want to eat it.

LOOKING FOR FOOD

Butterflies drink a sugary liquid called nectar for their food. Nectar is found in flowers.

Butterflies look for brightly coloured flowers to find nectar. They drink it using their tongues, which they use like a straw!

WORLD RECORD BREAKERS

The Skipper butterfly is faster than any Olympic runner.

Skipper Butterfly
The World's Fastest Butterfly
Top Speed:
30 miles per hour

23 24 25 26 27 28 29 30 31 32 33 34 35 36 37 38 39 40 41 42 43 44

Queen Alexandria Birdwing Butterfly
The World's Biggest Butterfly
Size:
25 cm

Some butterflies can be huge! See how big 25 cm is using the measuring tape shown.

LIFE CYCLE OF A BUTTERFLY

1 A butterfly lays an egg or eggs on a leaf.

2 Caterpillars hatch from of the butterfly's eggs.

LIFE CYCLES

3 A caterpillar changes into a hard chrysalis.

4 An adult butterfly breaks out of the chrysalis.

Get Exploring!

Can you spot any butterflies in your garden or local park?

The best time to look for butterflies is in the summer when it is warm and sunny. See how many different types of butterfly you can find.

GLOSSARY

chrysalis the hard shell that grows around a caterpillar's body
hatch when a young animal breaks out of its egg
insect a small animal that has six legs and four wings
sheds when an insect's old skin falls off

INDEX

caterpillars 8–14, 22
chrysalis 12–14, 22
eggs 6–8, 22
eggshells 8
insects 5
food 10, 15, 18
leaves: 6, 10, 17, 22
nectar 18–19
plants 6, 18

Queen Alexandria Birdwing butterfly 21
Skipper butterfly 20
wings 5, 15–17

PHOTO CREDITS

Photocredits: Abbreviations: l-left, r-right, b-bottom, t-top, c-centre, m-middle.
Front Cover — suns07butterfly. 1 – suns07butterfly, 2 – ilikestudio, 3t – ArchMan, 3m – PhotonCatcher, 3b – Kirsanov Valeriy Vladimirovich, 4l – Oksana Kuzmina, 4c – Ljupco Smokovski, 5 – ArchMan, 6 – MarkMirror, 6inset – Sarah2, 7tl – Pan Xunbin, 7tr – Pan Xunbin, 7bl – Henrik Larsson, 7br – Pan Xunbin , 8t – Valentyn Volkov, 8m – Cathy Keifer, 9tr – Tischenko Irina, 9ct – Eric Isselee, 9cm – Kirsanov Valeriy Vladimirovich, 9cb – alle, 10tr – Tischenko Irina, 10 ml – Eric Isselee, 11 tr – Tischenko Irina, 11m 56556355, 12 – PhotonCatcher, 13 – StevenRussellSmithPhotos, 14 – 173557913, 15 – 2nix Studio, 16 – Oleg_Z, 17 – Christopher Tan Teck Hean, 18 – ilikestudio, 19 – ATOM WANG, 20/21 – Nomad_Soul, 20back – 71537983, 20front – Valentyna Chukhlyebova, 21back – Svhl, 21front – jpsm, 22t – Sarah2, 22ml – Marcio Jose Bastos Silva, 22mr – Brandon Alms, 22b – 181345142, 23 – Ian Grainger, 24t – ArchMan, 24b – ilikestudio, Images are courtesy of Shutterstock.com. With thanks to Getty Images, Thinkstock Photo and iStockphoto.